Shapes

The Scribbles Institute™ *Young Artist Basics*

Published by The Child's World®
PO Box 326
Chanhassen, MN 55317-0326
800-599-READ
www.childsworld.com

Design and Production: The Creative Spark, San Juan Capistrano, CA
Series Editor: Elizabeth Sirimarco Budd

Photos:
© PhotoDisc/H. Wiesenhofer/PhotoLink: cover, 17
© 2002 Artists Rights Society (ARS), New York/VG Bild-Kunst, Bonn/Scala/Art
     Resource, NY: 30
© David M. Budd Photography: 11, 26
© 2002 Estate of Alexander Calder/Artists Rights Society (ARS), New York/Art
     Resource, NY: 13-14
© California Institute of Technology: 15
© Joe Arias De Cordoba: 29
© Erich Lessing/Art Resource, NY: 8
© Jamie Marshall/tribaleye.co.uk: 19
© 2002 Succession H. Matisse, Paris/Artists Rights Society (ARS), New York/New
     York Public Library/Art Resource, NY: 25
© The Newark Museum/Art Resource, NY: 20
© PhotoDisc/Fototeca Storica Nazionale: 23

Library of Congress Cataloging-in-Publication Data
Court, Robert, 1956–
  Shapes / by Rob Court.
       p. cm.
Includes index.
Summary: Simple text and cartoon characters introduce basic shapes and their use in artwork and architecture.
  ISBN 1-56766-096-7 (lib. bdg.)
  1. Art—Technique—Juvenile literature.
  [1. Shape. 2. Art—Technique.] I. Title.
  N7430 .C695 2002
  701'.8—dc21
                                              2001007643

Shapes

Rob Court

Loopi is a line,
a fantastic line.

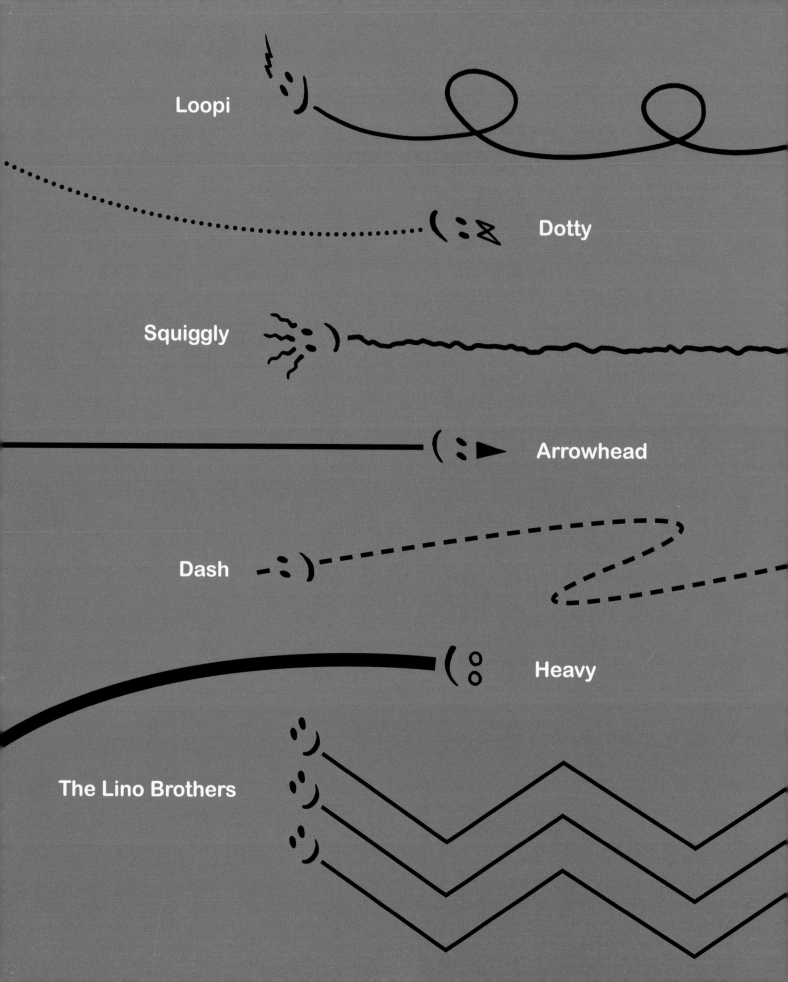

Loopi

Dotty

Squiggly

Arrowhead

Dash

Heavy

The Lino Brothers

There are many kinds of lines.

Some are dotted lines.

Some are squiggly lines.

Some lines point in a direction.

Some lines are drawn with dashes.

Other lines are very, very thick.

Sometimes lines work together
to make shapes.

Long ago, people used shapes to make stories with pictures. In ancient times, people often used shapes or symbols to **represent** things.

When a straight line bends, it becomes a curved line. When the ends of a curved line meet, it becomes a circle. A circle is a shape.

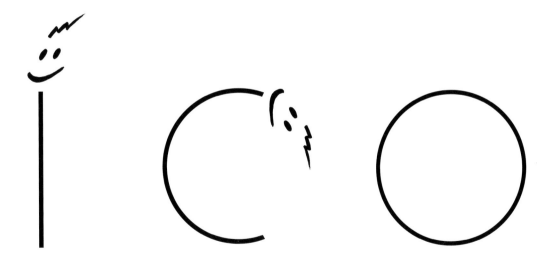

The symbols in this picture were made more than 3,000 years ago. An artist from Egypt created them on a stone wall. How many circles can you find in the picture? Can you think of different things a circle can represent?

Today, in countries all around the world, people use shapes as symbols. Symbols can be used to pass on important messages.

Right: What do these symbols tell you? What shapes do you see?

Below: This red symbol is an octagon. What do you think this symbol could mean?

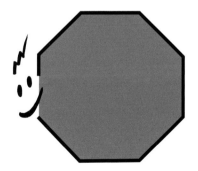

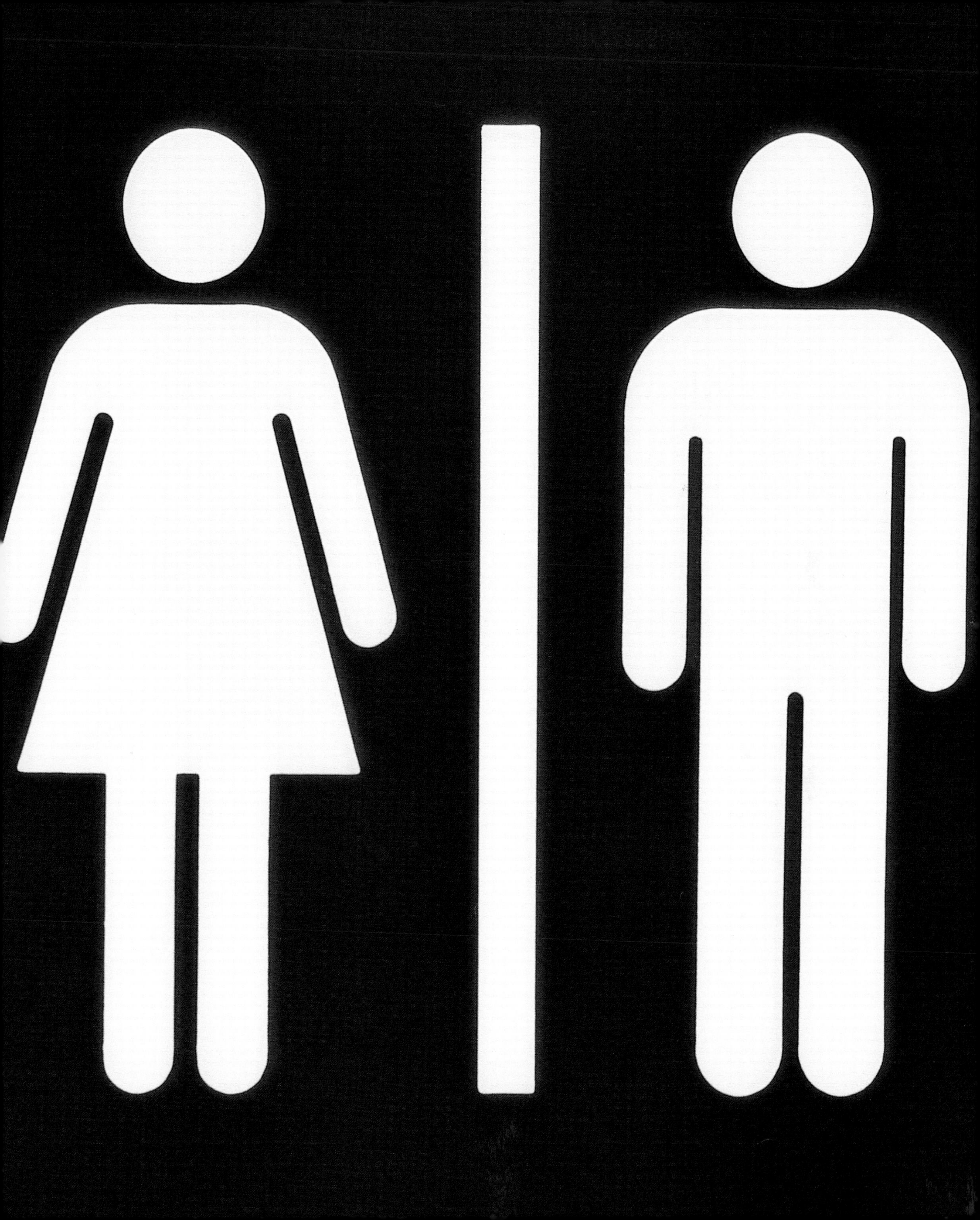

Artists can use shapes when they create **abstract art.**

Alexander Calder was an artist who made **mobiles** with different shapes. He used materials such as steel and paint.

How many circles do you see? Which circle is the smallest? Which circle is the largest? Do you see straight and curved lines?

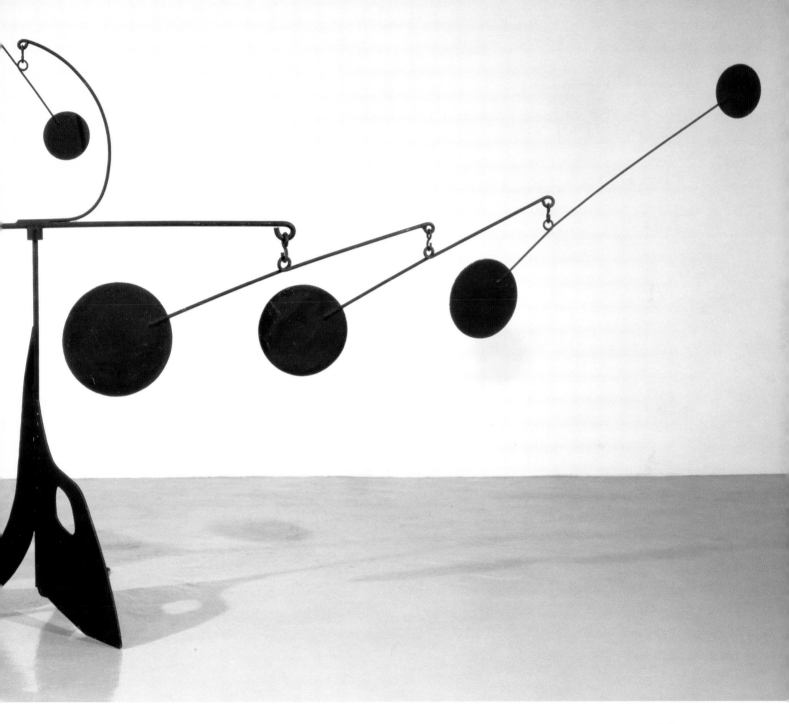

Alexander Calder, *Myxomatose,* 1953. Metal and steel.
This mobile is more than eight feet tall!

Some shapes are made by people. Other shapes are made by nature. If you look closely at things in nature, you can see many shapes.

A microscope is a tool that helps us see very small things. This is a picture of a snowflake taken through a microscope. Can you see different shapes in the snowflake?

Dotty can help you see that the left side of the snowflake looks the same as the right side. A shape that is balanced like this is a **symmetrical** shape.

14

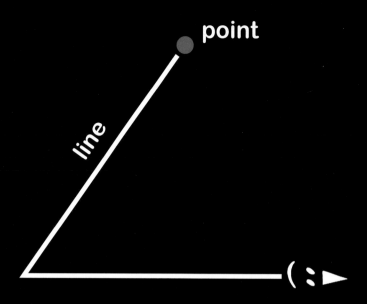

Arrowhead shows you that a **geometric** shape begins with a point. If you move a point from one place to another, it makes a line. When the lines are connected, they make a shape. Do you see a triangle?

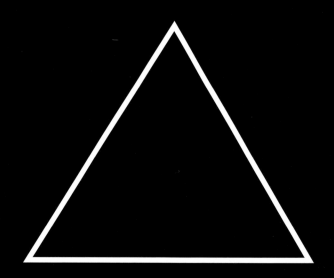

Look all around. You can see many
geometric shapes.

Artists in many countries use fabric to make art. For hundreds of years, artists in Honduras have used shapes to decorate fabric. This Honduran blanket is decorated with a bird.

Can you see how the artist used shapes and lines to create the bird? What shapes can you find? Do you see straight lines and angled lines?

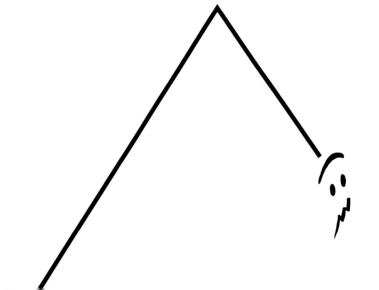

People in the United States use fabric to make art, too. A quilt is a blanket made with fabric shapes. The quiltmaker cuts out the shapes with scissors. A quilt is a beautiful piece of art that keeps you warm.

If you move a line from one side to another, it can make the shape of a square. All four sides of a square are the same.

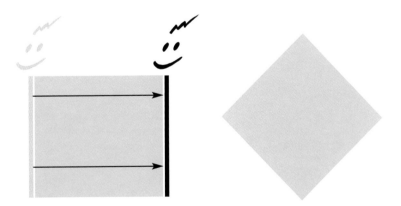

If you balance a square on one point, it makes the shape of a diamond. How many diamonds can you count in the quilt?

A rectangle is another shape with four sides. It is different from a square. On a rectangle, two sides are long, and two sides are short.

Can you find Loopi and Dotty in the painting? What shape do they make?

When a geometric shape is repeated, it can make a pattern. What shapes are used to make the pattern on the floor? How many rooms do you see?

Vittore Carpaccio, *Birth of Mary,* 1504–1508. Tempera on canvas.

Some shapes are not geometric.
You can cut out colored paper
to create a pretty **collage** with
different shapes.

The artist Henri Matisse made this collage with colored paper. Look at
the blue space around the black shape. What does the black shape
look like? Look at the red shape inside the black shape. What does the
red shape represent? How is this picture different from the picture on
page 11? How is it the same?

Can you find a yellow shape that looks like Dotty?

Henri Matisse, *Icarus,* **1947. Collage.**

The shape of a leaf is not geometric. It is not made by people, either. It is a natural shape. You can see the edge of the leaf against the dark background. Look hard at the edge of the leaf. This will help you draw a picture of it.

Can you draw the leaf from memory? Try moving your finger slowly around the edge of the leaf. Try to remember the shape as you do this. Now close the book. Draw the leaf on a sheet of paper.

An **architect** uses shapes to draw a plan for a house. Looking at a plan is like flying over a house without a roof on it. Can you see triangles? Can you see squares and circles?

An oval is a shape that looks like a circle squeezed together on both sides. Compare the oval shown below with the shapes in the plan. Where do you see an oval? Does the oval represent something in the house?

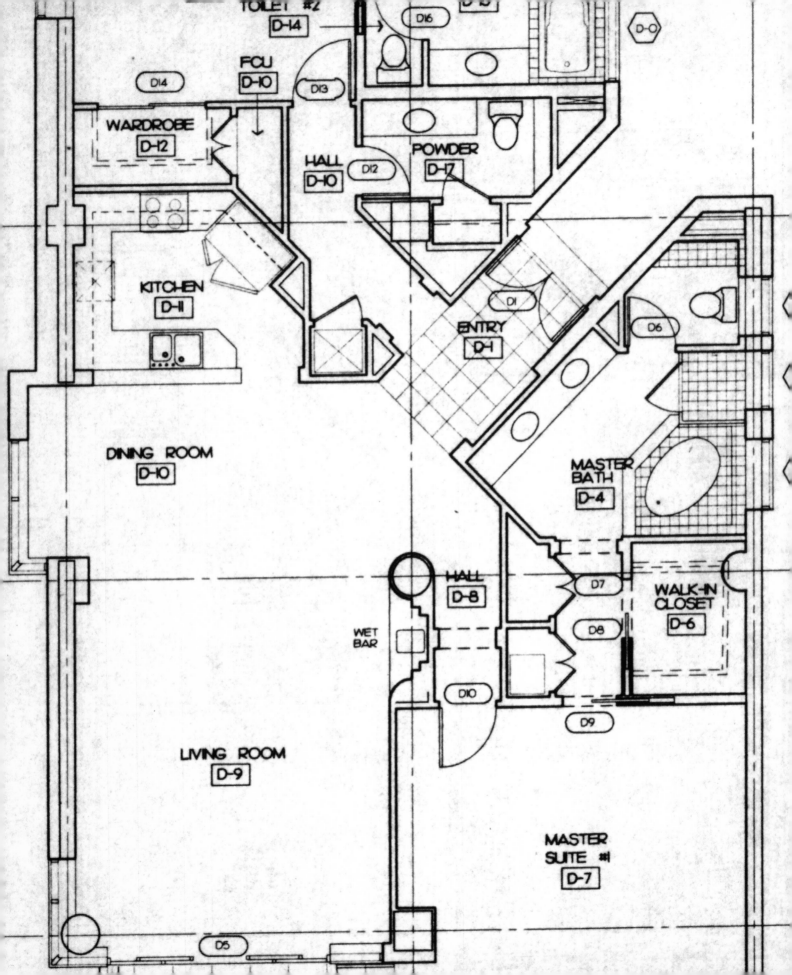

Paul Klee, *Senecio,* **1922. Oil on canvas.**

This painting was made by the artist Paul Klee. He used many shapes and colors to create a face.